How To Make Your Own Scarecrows

By Mary Kay Fisher

How to Make Your Own Scarecrows

Printed in the United States of America

ISBN 0-9895841-0-0

Photographs by Mary Kay Fisher, David A. Stuart, Rex Rose, Eleanor Catalano, Mary Lister
Illustrations by Mary Kay Fisher

Library of Congress Cataloging-in-Publication Data

Dedication

This book is dedicated to the Buchanan, Michigan "Scarecrow Ladies" whose friendship, energy and creativity never cease to amaze and inspire me.

Preface

I have been making scarecrows every fall since 1987 and had always thought of them as lifeless stuffed creatures with outstretched arms and scary faces. Then I met Carole Hedstrom. Carole showed me how to make scarecrows come to life by posing them doing something like everyday people doing everyday things.

This book is a composite of some of the scarecrows constructed in past years. The ideas in this book are intended to give you the guidelines needed for making your own personal scarecrows. Have fun using your creativity in bringing your own charming scarecrow to life!

Mary

Contents

Introduction

All of the scarecrows pictured in this book were created by a group of volunteers in Buchanan, Michigan—usually referred to as "the Scarecrow Ladies." In reality, these ladies are a non-profit organization called Buchanan Scarecrow Charities. Each year these volunteers raise funds by making scarecrows to sell to local businesses. These scarecrows are then displayed for two months in the downtown business area. Well over 100 scarecrows are featured each year.

This fall display of stuffed creatures has become tradition for the small Michigan town. People come from all over to have lunch, walk around town, take pictures, and view the scarecrows.

The best part is the money gained from the sale of these scarecrows stays right in the Buchanan community! Funds are provided for: the local food pantry, college scholarships, Buchanan High School enrichment programs, Buchanan Art Center special projects, Buchanan Public Library needs, and other community organizations and individual needs.

The Buchanan District Library used this Henry VIII scarecrow as an educational opportunity with this display.

Before You Begin

Careful planning before you start making your scarecrow will cut down on frustration and make creating your scarecrow a pleasant and fun experience.

First decide:

1. Where are you going to place your scarecrow? Your scarecrow cannot stand alone. It will need to be tied to something such as a lamp post or porch railing in order to keep it from falling over. A sitting scarecrow can be placed in a chair or on a porch step, but still needs to be securely anchored so that it will not fall over when strong winds blow.

2. How big do you want your scarecrow to be? Adult size scarecrows can be very unwieldy and heavy to handle. A better choice would be a scarecrow made from women's size small clothes.

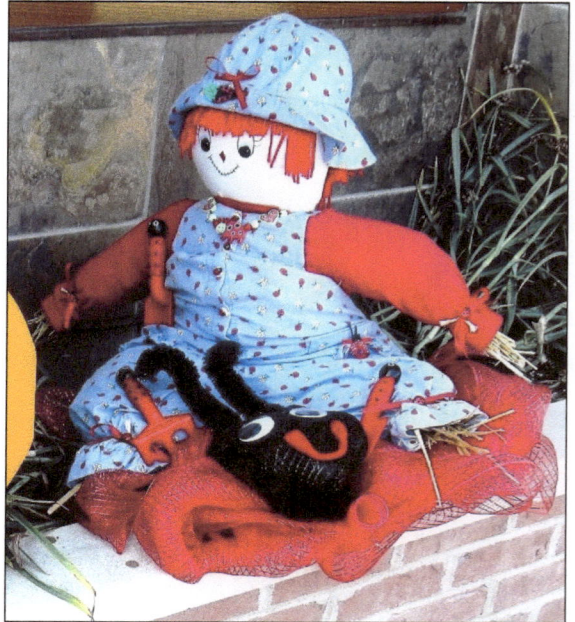

3. Do you want your scarecrow to stand up straight or do you want to have it sit? The type of wooden frame used will depend upon how you want your scarecrow to be positioned. A full length frame is needed for a scarecrow that will stand while a half frame is used for a scarecrow that needs to bend at the waist.

4. Are you going to make a male or a female scarecrow?

Female scarecrows do not always need a dress, but if a dress is to be used, it needs to be placed over a scarecrow body that has been constructed using bib overalls and a long sleeve shirt. If desired, denim legs can be covered by pulling colored tights over the legs.

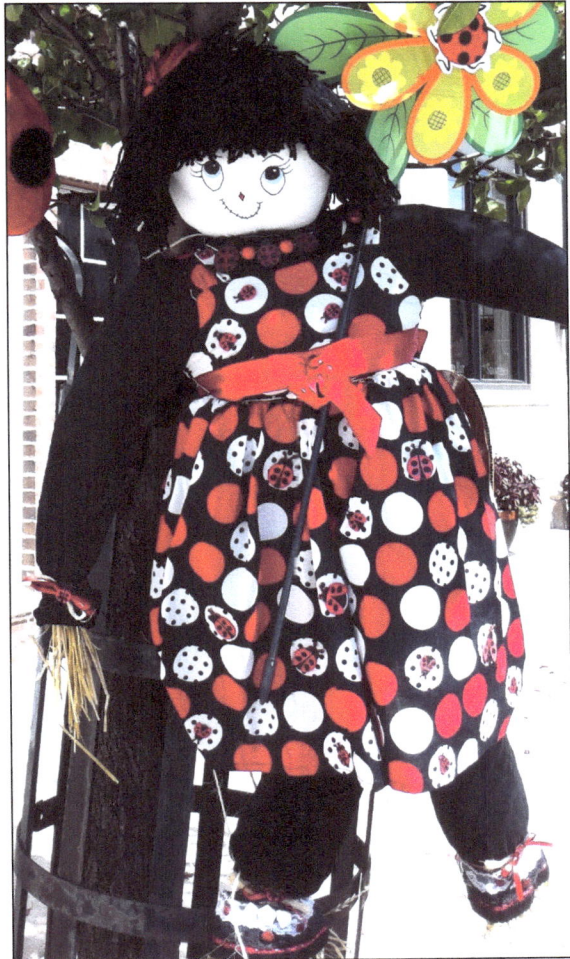

General Supplies

Materials

- **Wood:** 1"x 2" piece of wood for scarecrow frame. This wood usually comes in 8 foot lengths. Depending upon the size and type of frame to be constructed, one 8 foot piece and one 4 foot piece would be more than enough for one 6 foot scarecrow.

- **Fabric for head:** Approximately a fourth yard of fabric is needed for the scarecrow head. Suggested fabrics are: muslin, an old pillow case, light colored cotton, or burlap.

- **Thread** to match head fabric

- **Polyester Fiberfill:** The completed sewn head is stuffed with polyester fiberfill instead of straw. Fiberfill will give the head a firm rounded shape and will stay clean in any kind of weather. A head stuffed with straw can become misshapen over time and will become soiled when left out in the rain. Approximately one pound of fiberfill is needed for a large scarecrow head.

- **Clothes:** A long-sleeve shirt and bib overalls are the basic clothes for a scarecrow. However, many variations of this combination are possible

  Bib overalls (or some type of full body coverall) are necessary in order to contain the straw inside the scarecrow body and to help keep the total figure together.

A woven fabric long sleeve shirt should be used as a knit shirt will totally stretch out of proportion as it is stuffed.

(*See overstuffed scarecrow below*)

If you want to use something such as a knit turtle-neck shirt or a dress, first construct a basic scarecrow using a woven fabric long-sleeve shirt and bib overalls, then pull the knit shirt or dress over the scarecrow completing the look you desire.

Usually adult size clothes make a bulky, unwieldy scarecrow. To avoid this problem, choose either small women, teen, or large child size clothes. Small, child sizes make adorable little scarecrows.

- **Hair:** The possibilities of what material to choose for hair are endless. Yarn, raffia, paper twist, torn rags, rope, old wigs and t-shirt strips are good choices.

  DO NOT choose a string mop for hair if your scarecrow will be outside. Rain will completely soak strings in the mop causing the head to be extremely heavy and fall forward.

- **Hat:** A traditional scarecrow wears a straw hat. Do not be limited by this tradition. Scarecrows can wear ball caps, felt hats, fancy hats, hard hats, any hat you desire.

  Should you not want your scarecrow to wear a hat, cover the top of the head with whatever material you have chosen for hair.

- **Silk Flowers, scarf, fabric patches, etc.** Use these items and more to embellish your scarecrow.

- **Straw:** Straw is a great material for stuffing scarecrows. It easily maintains the body shape and dries out quickly should a rainstorm soak your scarecrow. A half bale would be more than enough to stuff a large scarecrow.

General Supplies

Tools

- **Wood saw:** Either a powered or hand saw is needed to cut wood into desired lengths for scarecrow frame.

- **Screwdriver and 1 1/8" or 1 5/8" drywall screws:** Use to screw scarecrow frame together.

- **Staple gun and staples:** Use to staple completed scarecrow cloth head to wooden frame.

- **Hot glue gun and glue sticks:** Hot glue is used to adhere hair to the scarecrow head and to add embellishments such as colorful patches, silk flowers, etc.

- **Scissors**

- **Sewing Machine:** use to sew head pieces together.

- **Yardstick or measuring tape**

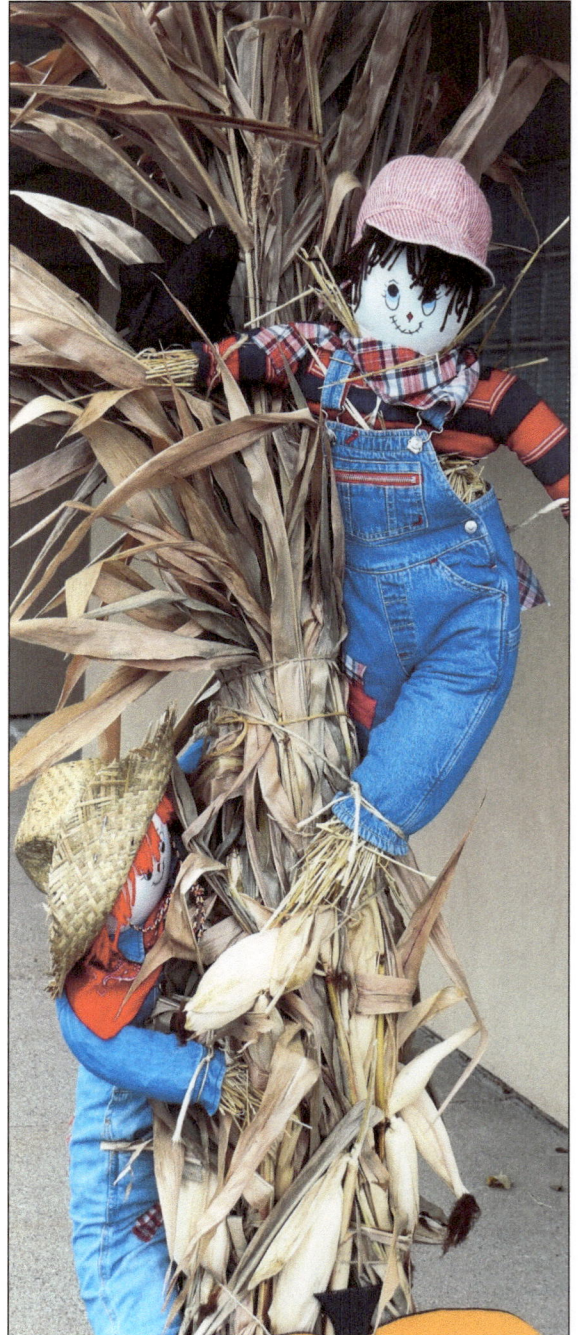

Miscellaneous Supplies

- **Graphite Paper:** Transfer face pattern onto head material with graphite paper.

- **Thin line black permanent marker:** A thin line permanent marker is used to draw the face. It must contain permanent ink, particularly if your scarecrow will be outside in the elements.

- **Small artist paint brushes.** Use to paint eyes and nose

- **Acrylic Paint:** Light blue, black, red, and white paint is used to paint eyes and nose. Light brown paint is needed for freckles.

- **Twine:** Twine is needed to tie scarecrow head, arms and legs.

- **Cornstalks:** Although not necessary, cornstalks placed behind a scarecrow add a special fall touch. Not many are needed.

- **Props:** The addition of props can add a whole new dimension to your scarecrow display. Throughout this book you will notice how the Scarecrow Ladies use various props to create a scene.

Scarecrow Construction

Head Construction

1. Cut three head pattern pieces from chosen fabric. Using graphite paper, copy scarecrow face onto first head section.

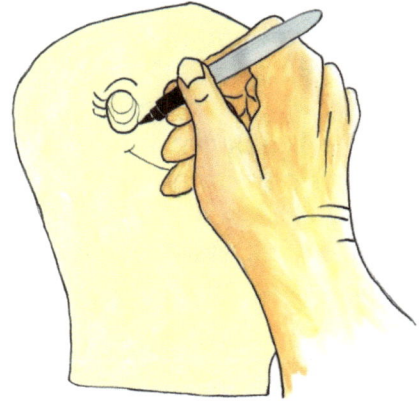

2. With a thin black permanent marker trace graphite lines of eyes, nose, mouth, eyebrows and eyelashes.

3. Paint iris of eye light blue. Let dry. Paint nose red. Let dry. Paint pupil black. Let dry. Add a white dot for highlight in pupil of each eye. Let dry.

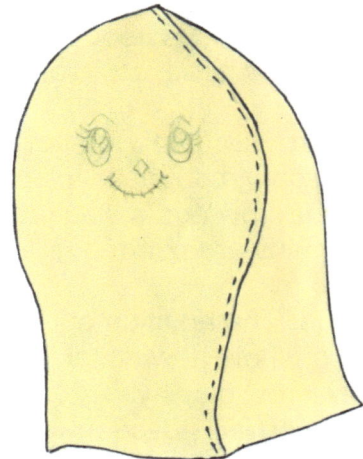

4. With right sides together sew two head pieces together as shown.

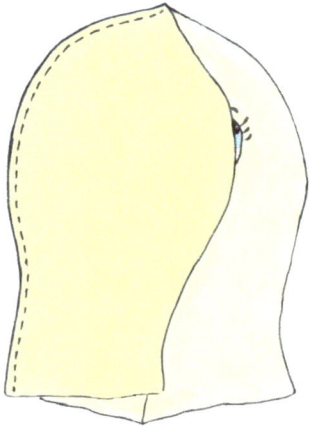

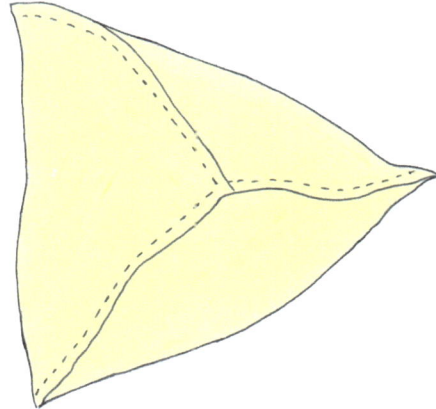

5. Sew third head piece to this assembly in the same manner.

6. Sew first and third head pieces together forming complete head. Turn right side out.

Frame Construction

If a traditional standing scarecrow is desired, use a full length frame. Use a half frame for a sitting scarecrow that can be posed with arms and legs that can be bent into position. In either case the completed scarecrow will need to be fastened to something such as a pole, post, chair or garden hook to secure it in place in an upright position.

Standing scarecrow full length frame

1. Using 1" x 2" wood, cut body stick 19 inches longer than the measurement from bib overalls shoulder to bottom of leg. The top 7 inches will extend into the head while the bottom 12 inches will extend out of the pant legs and will keep the scarecrow up off the ground.

7 inches

length of bib overalls

12 inches

2. Cut second piece of wood (shoulder stick) the width of the shirt from cuff to cuff. **Note:** If a standing scarecrow with movable arms is desired cut a shorter stick measuring from shoulder seam to shoulder seam as shown on the next page.

Assemble Frame

7 inches

Using two screws join shoulder stick 7 inches down from the top of the body stick.

Sitting Scarecrow Frame Construction

Sitting or posable scarecrow half-frame

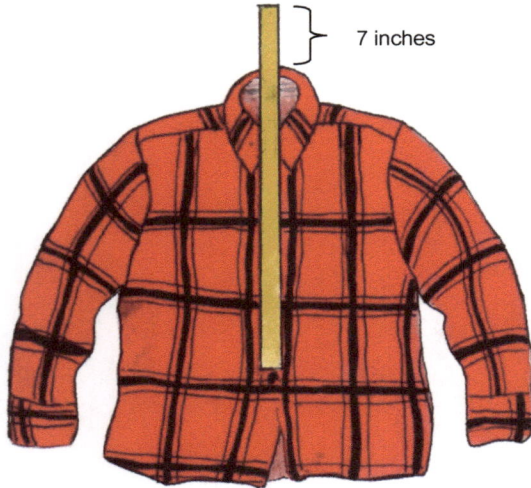

7 inches

1. Using 1" x 2" stick cut body stick 7 inches longer than the measurement from waist to shoulder.

2. Cut second piece of wood (shoulder stick) the width of the shirt from shoulder seam to shoulder seam.

Assemble Frame

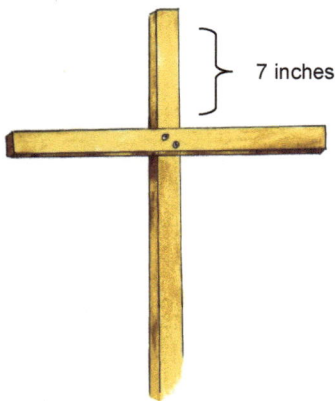

7 inches

Using two screws join shoulder stick 7 inches down from the top of the body stick.

Stuff Head

1. Slip completed head assembly over top of wooden frame. Stuff with polyester batting until firm and rounded. Pull fabric down at bottom of sewn head and staple to shoulder stick front and back.

2. To make head more secure tie a piece of twine around bottom of head and around wooden frame crisscrossing front to back.

3. Bottoms of plastic water bottles are used to form the shoulder. These bottle bottoms prevent the shoulder stick from poking through the stuffed straw creating an unnatural pointed shoulder. Cut ends off of two plastic bottles. Staple one cut bottle bottom on each end of shoulder stick.

Stuff Body

1. Slip shirt over frame and button front completely.

2. Using handfuls of straw, start stuffing in shoulder areas of shirt both front and back. Push straw down sleeve from inside of shirt. Then push straw up sleeve from cuff. If necessary use a stick to push straw into the shirt sleeves. Continue to stuff shirt until upper body is rounded and firm. Tie bottom of shirt tightly around body stick. This will keep the straw in the upper body and will prevent it from gravitating down into the overalls.

3. Allow about 8 to 10 inches of straw to stick out of wrist cuff. Tie sleeve tightly at cuff to keep straw secure.

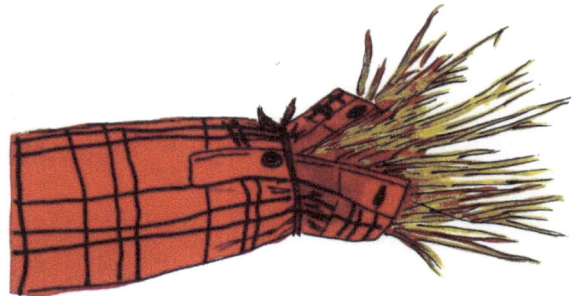

1. If using long body stick for standing scarecrow, slip one leg of bib overalls through bottom of body stick. Pull up, tucking stuffed shirt into pants. Place straps over scarecrow shoulders and fasten in front.

   If using short body stick for sitting scarecrow, pull overalls over the bottom of the stuffed shirt. Pull straps around back of stuffed shirt and fasten in front.

2. Firmly stuff top part of overalls front and back. Then push handfuls of straw up pant legs. Use a stick to push straw firmly into pant legs.

   Continue to use more straw to stuff and shape scarecrow until it is the shape and firmness desired.

3. Allow about 8 to 10 inches of straw to stick out bottom of pant legs. When legs are firmly stuffed, tie securely at bottom with twine.

Hats

After your scarecrow is firmly stuffed, it is time to choose a hat. You do not need to be limited to a straw hat. Any hat that will withstand the elements will do. Your choice of hat will determine where and how your scarecrow hair will be glued to the stuffed head.

1. Place hat on scarecrow head. Draw a light pencil line on stuffed head just under the brim to indicate placement of hair.

2. Set hat aside and proceed to hair section.

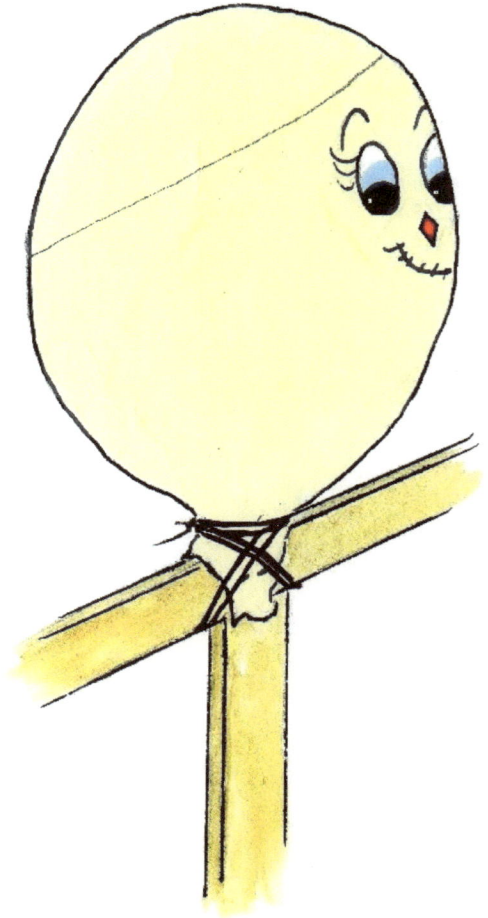

Hair

Now that you have chosen a hat for your scarecrow, it is time to choose the kind of hair you would like to use. The possibilities of material for hair are endless. Recommended choices include: yarn, rope, raffia, paper twist, torn rags, t-shirt strips and even old wigs.

(**DO NOT** choose a string mop if your scarecrow will be outside. Rain will totally soak the mop causing the head to be extremely heavy and fall forward.)

Hair

Yarn Hair

The colors and varieties of yarn provide the scarecrow maker with a smorgasbord of choices for scarecrow hair.

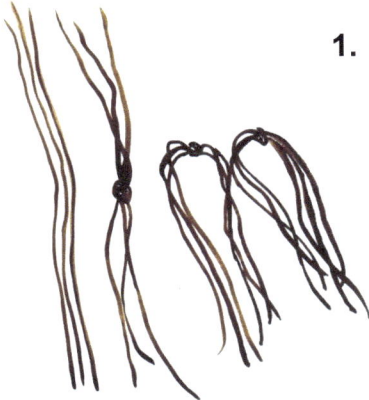

1. For short hair, cut yarn in 5 inch lengths. For longer hair, cut yarn two times the desired hair length. Tie 3 strands of yarn together in the middle.

2. Hot glue each tied yarn section side by side along pencil guideline on stuffed head.

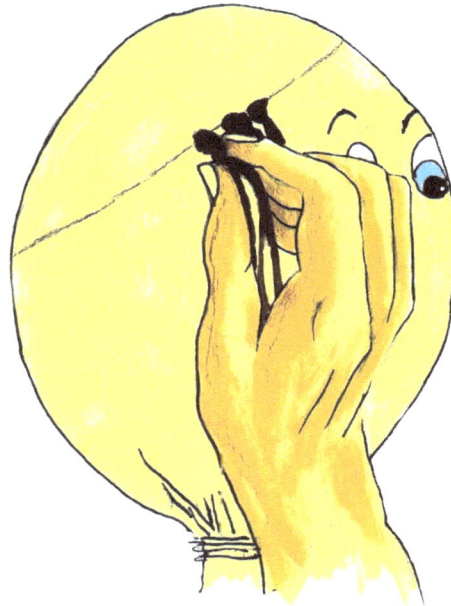

3. Trim yarn to desired length and style. Cut bangs above eyebrows. Trim hair sides and back

Hair

Yarn Hair

Yarn is an easy and inexpensive material to use for hair. It can be styled in various ways—long, short, braids, ponytails, etc.

Yarn Hair

The yarn hair on the two scarecrows at left is created by entirely covering head with short, tied strands of yarn.

Hair

Rope Hair

Rope is an excellent material to use for scarecrow hair. It not only has a very natural look, but is sturdy and holds up well in wind and rain. One can find rope in a variety of natural brown colors.

Rope Hair

Rope hair is prepared similarly to yarn hair, except that rope hair needs to be separated into individual strands. Strands will be curly.

To prepare rope hair, first cut rope into desired lengths. Next separate each length into individual strands. Tie about three strands together in the middle as shown above.

Attach to scarecrow head as shown in yarn hair section on page 27.

Hair

T-Shirt Strip Hair

1. Lay t-shirt on flat surface. With scissors cut one inch wide strips across bottom of t-shirt. Cut each strip in half.

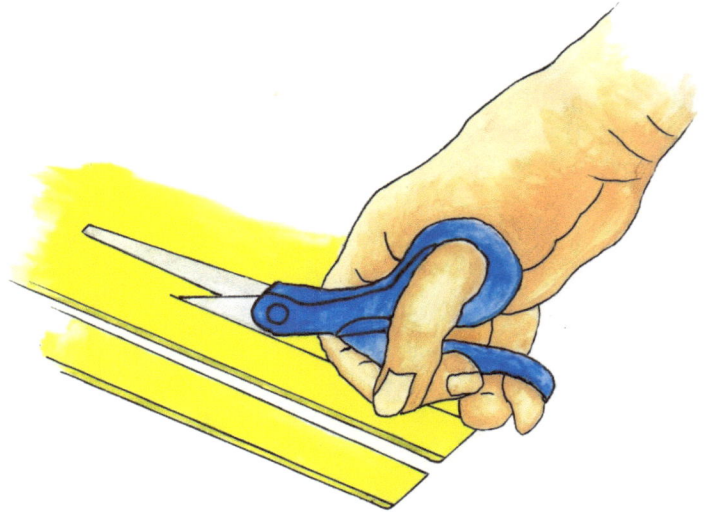

2. Pick up t-shirt strip and pull at each end. This will cause the knit fabric to curl slightly.

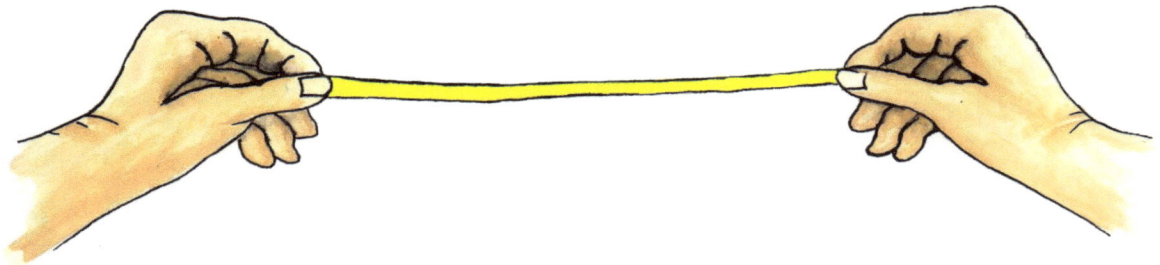

3. Tie each strip in the middle with a single knot. Glue each knotted t-shirt strip at hat placement line. Trim t-shirt strip hair to desired length.

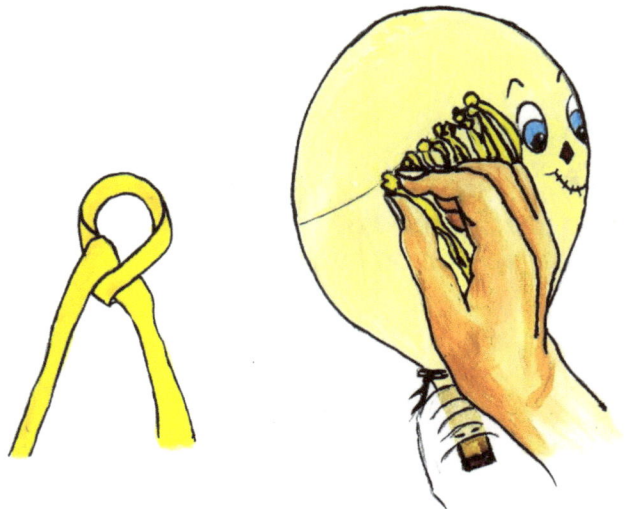

T-Shirt Strip

Hair

Raffia Hair

1. Gather small bunches of raffia together and tie in the middle with a single knot.

2. Glue each tied section front to back down center of stuffed head.

3. Part raffia hair in the middle at the back of the head. Gather all raffia together on either side of the scarecrow head if desired and tie with a ribbon. Otherwise allow raffia hair to hang down over shoulders and back.

Raffia Hair

Hair

Paper Twist Hair

Paper twist is wonderful to use as scarecrow hair. It has the look of corn stalk leaves and corn husks. there are many colors and widths of paper twist from which to choose. A four inch width was used in the illustrations on this page. If using a wider width, adjust construction accordingly.

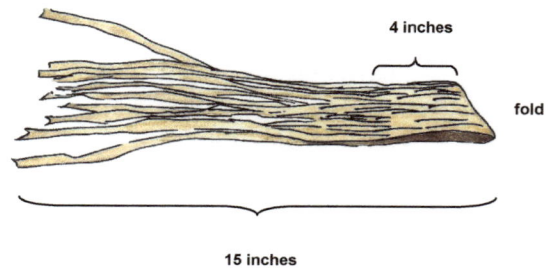

1. Cut paper twist into four 30 inch lengths. Unravel each section.

2. Fold in half. Cut narrow strips up to the last 4 inches. Unfold each section.

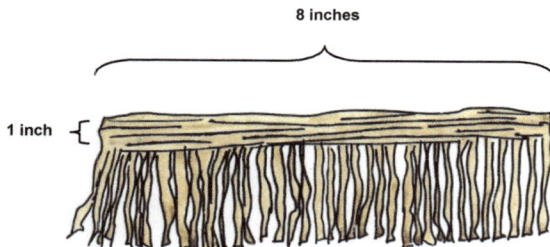

3. For bangs cut paper twist into an 8 inch length. Unravel. Cut narrow strips across paper twist as shown leaving the last inch intact.

4. Hot glue two of the unfolded 30 inch sections across top of stuffed scarecrow head.

5. Cut remaining two of the 30 inch sections in half. Hot glue each section to back of head.

6. Glue strip for bangs across top of head. Trim all hair to desired length.

Hair

Paper Twist Hair

Crafts using paper twist were very popular in past years. It can still be found in various craft stores and through the Internet.

Because light beige paper twist is the color of dried cornstalks it is a good color for scarecrow hair. Do not be limited to this color, however. Using yellow or orange paper twist can add brightness and color to your scarecrow.

Paper Twist Hair

Hair

Torn Rags Hair

The ripped effect of torn cloth gives a great look to scarecrow hair as it can look old and weathered.

Rip colorful woven cloth into inch wide strips. The length of the hair will be determined by the length of the fabric. **Note:** Do not use knit fabric as it will not tear.

If your scarecrow is going to wear a hat, tie a single knot in the center of each torn strip and glue to stuffed head as shown in the yarn section on page 27.

If your scarecrow is not going to have a hat, the torn rags need to cover the entire head.
Start out by cutting short strips and gluing them across the forehead to form bangs as shown.

Torn Rags Hair

Next, cover the glued ends of the
bangs by finding the middle of each
strip and systematically gluing each
strip side by side (as shown) until entire
stuffed head is covered.

Hair

Wigs

Wig hair is the easiest hair to use. Just glue the wig onto scarecrow head and comb into desired style.

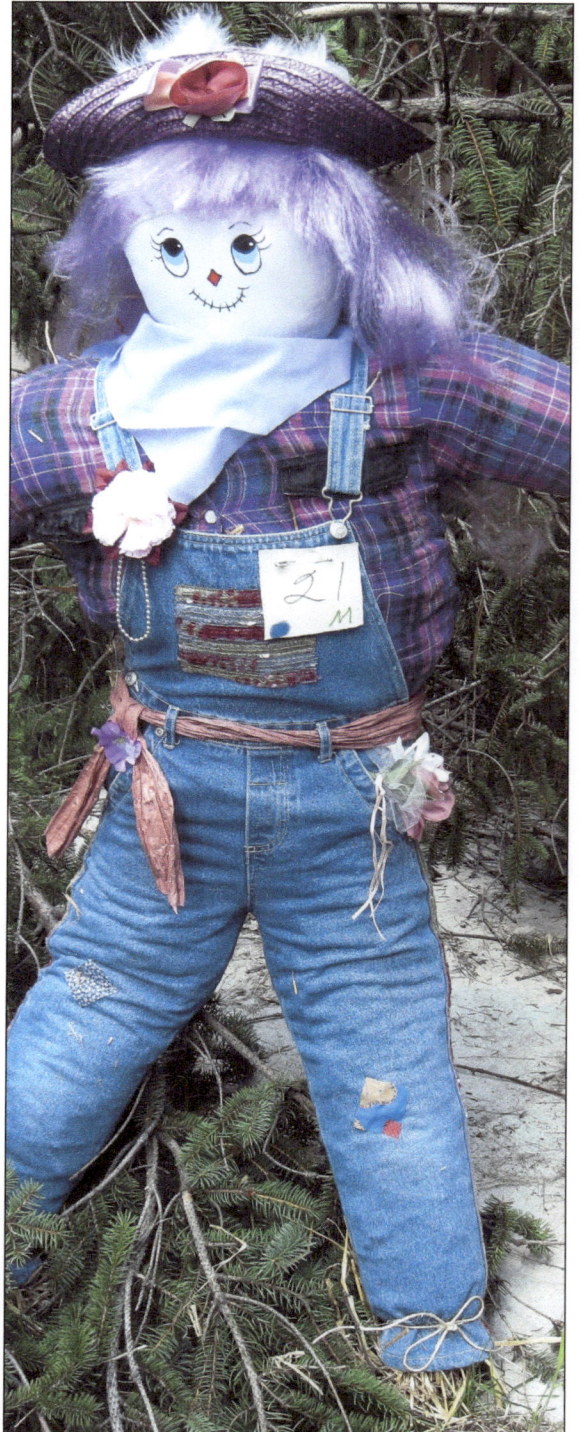

Hair

Painted hair

Pierrot the clown and these cartoon characters only need hair that is painted directly onto their stuffed head.

Using a pencil, draw a guide line around the head indicating where the hair should be.

Using acrylic paint, paint area enclosed by pencil line.

Hair

Braids

Cover head with desired hair material which has been cut twice the length of desired braid length. Part hair in the back. Gather hair (front to mid-back) on one side of the head. Divide strands into three parts and braid to desired length. Tie braid at the end with colorful ribbon. Do the same for other side.

Freckles

Freckles are not symmetrical and are different sizes and shapes. Use a medium brown or medium reddish brown paint.

The key to making freckles is to randomly make them different sizes and space them unevenly over the cheek area. Do not space them evenly apart.

Beards and Mustaches

A sharp black or dark brown eyebrow pencil is a great tool for making beard stubble. It is waterproof so is perfect should your scarecrow be out in the elements. Make short marks and dots all over the lower portion of the face as shown above.

Beards and Mustaches

Beards and mustaches can be made of wigs, yarn, macramé cord, felt, etc.

Accessories

Scarves

Now it is time to add those little touches that make your scarecrow unique. A simple scarf tied around the neck adds color and interest. Scarves can be tied in the front, side, or back.

Make a scarf out of a triangular piece of cloth, or just a wide strip of fabric. Use bright colors.

Accessories

Patches and handkerchiefs

Glue colorful fabric patches to shirt and pants.

A bright colored handkerchief or scrap of cloth tucked into a front or back pocket adds color and interest.

Glasses

Glasses can add a mysterious or studious look; even a wild and crazy look!

Accessories

Gloves

There are times when gloves are important to complete the desired look for a scarecrow. When using gloves it is easier to stuff each finger firmly with fiberfill than to stuff with straw.

This "wannabe" rock star scarecrow needs a white glove to complete his ensemble.

Gloves are a "must" to make this royal wave authentic.

Shoes

Not too many scarecrows wear shoes, but do not let that deter you from putting a pair on your scarecrow. Roller skates on the scarecrow at right makes this "car hop" look authentic as do the "waders" on the fisherman below.

Accessories

Leaves, fall flowers, ribbons, and more

Imitation grapes add a nice touch to this straw hat.

Imitation fall leaves are a perfect addition to a straw hat. Not only are they colorful, they hold up well in the unpredictable fall weather.

Fall colors of red, yellow, orange, and brown do not always have to be used. The scarecrow at left is splendid in purple and lavender with touches of pink ribbon around the wrists and purple ribbon to adorn the hat.

Add a band of color and some bright flowers or leaves to wrists and straw hat.

Decorate tied wrists and ankles with ribbon, gathered fabric, or anything else you might desire.

Beads, flowers and ribbons make the little scarecrow at right very stylish.

Props

Props add a wonderful dimension to scarecrows. They help define the scene you wish to portray.

This shepherd girl's sheep was made by covering a Christmas deer frame with tufts of polyester fiberfill. Ears were made of white felt. The white staff adds to the scene.

This hobo scarecrow has more character with his knapsack of treasures, pots and pans, and soup cans.

The aluminum wash tub and bubble wrap stuffed inside to simulate bubbles completes the scene of these three "rub a dub dub" scarecrows in a tub.

Props

Boxing gloves and a towel add a touch of realism to the prizefighter scarecrow above while the frog at right (which was stuffed with straw) completes the scene of the princess and the frog.

This adorable little boy scarecrow looks even cuter with his pet dog. When using a large stuffed animal as a prop take out the inside stuffing and replace with straw. This helps the animal "tie in" with the fall scarecrow theme and also will dry out fast after a rainstorm.

The ladder and the wooden apples hanging in the tree are needed for this scarecrow apple pickers display.

The visor, golf club and golf shoes definitely make this lady scarecrow's outfit complete.

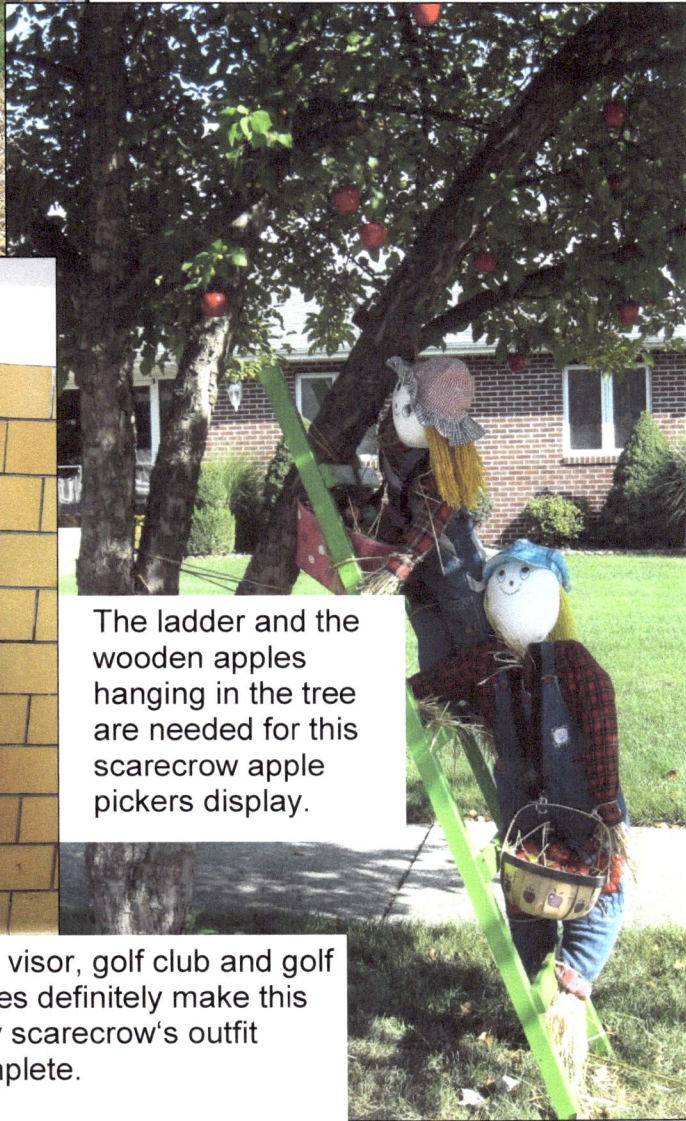

59

Props

This charming farmer scarecrow looks like he just left the chicken coop after gathering eggs.

Every fireman scarecrow needs a Dalmatian.

The props in these three pictures identify the characters portrayed. Moses is easily recognized by the Ten Commandments tablets and his staff, while puppies and a white coat give the impression of a Veterinarian. A megaphone and school letter clearly depict a cheerleader.

Displaying

Standing scarecrows

How you display your scarecrow is as important as how you construct it. A lot of time and effort went into making your scarecrow; how you display it will add the final touch. If your scarecrow was made with a full frame to make it stand, you will be limited to placing the arms and one leg in different positions. The scarecrows on these two pages suggest different ways to pose a standing scarecrow

The two scarecrows below stand up very straight. The way their arms are positioned adds interest to their display.

Standing scarecrows

The mother scarecrow below cradles a baby in one arm and holds onto a toddler with the other arm.

The scarecrow above was tied high off the ground with one arm flung over the arm of a lamp post.

Displaying

Half-frame scarecrows

Because the scarecrows on these two pages were constructed with a half-frame it was possible to position them in various poses. These scarecrows are able to bend at the waist and both arms and legs can be moved into various positions.

Half-frame scarecrows

Panoramas

Each year the Scarecrow Ladies create a special display at the city of Buchanan entrance sign. The theme is kept secret until the panorama is erected in early fall. These four scenes are examples of displays constructed in past years.

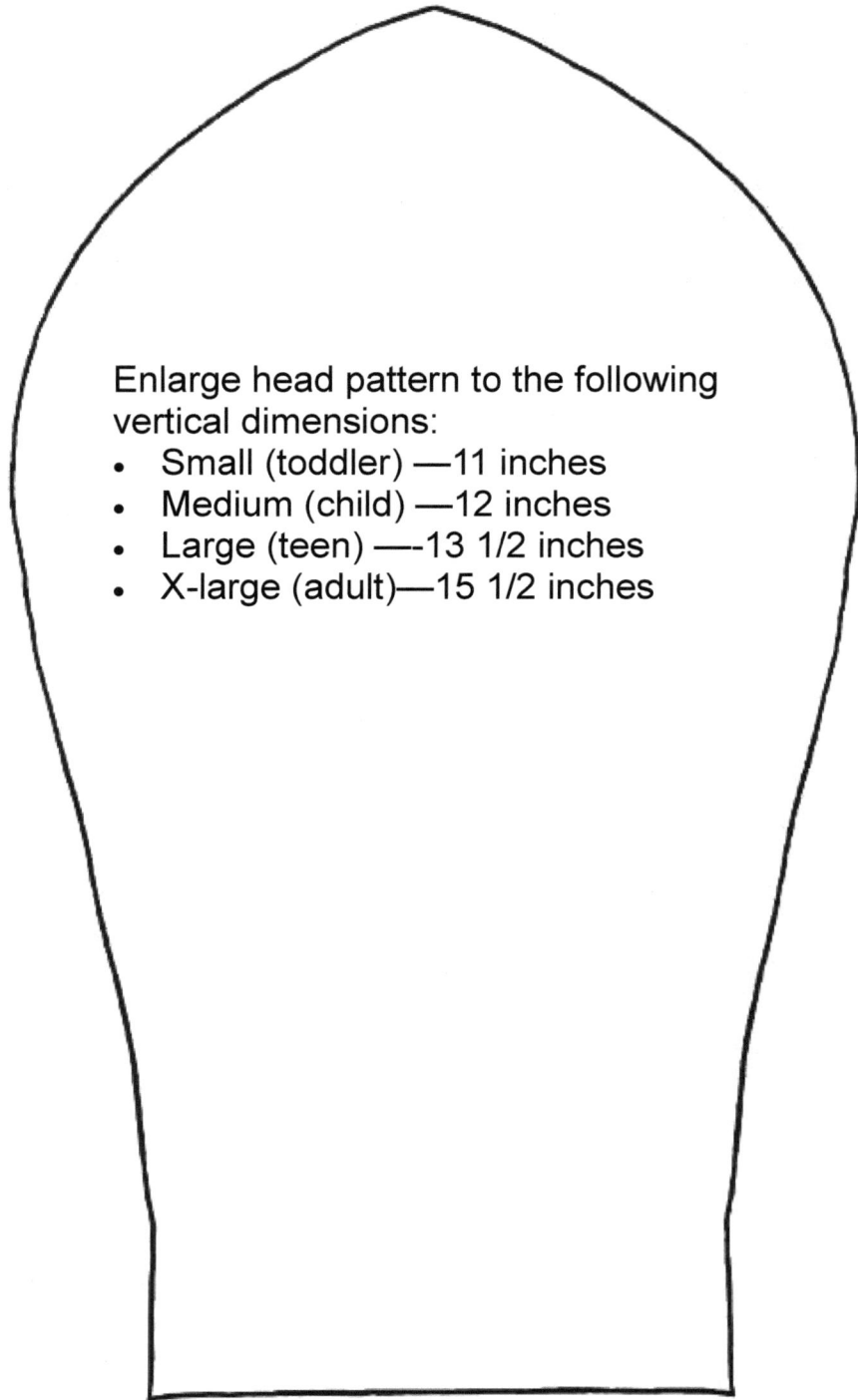

Patterns

Enlarge head pattern to the following
vertical dimensions:
- Small (toddler) —11 inches
- Medium (child) —12 inches
- Large (teen) —-13 1/2 inches
- X-large (adult)—15 1/2 inches

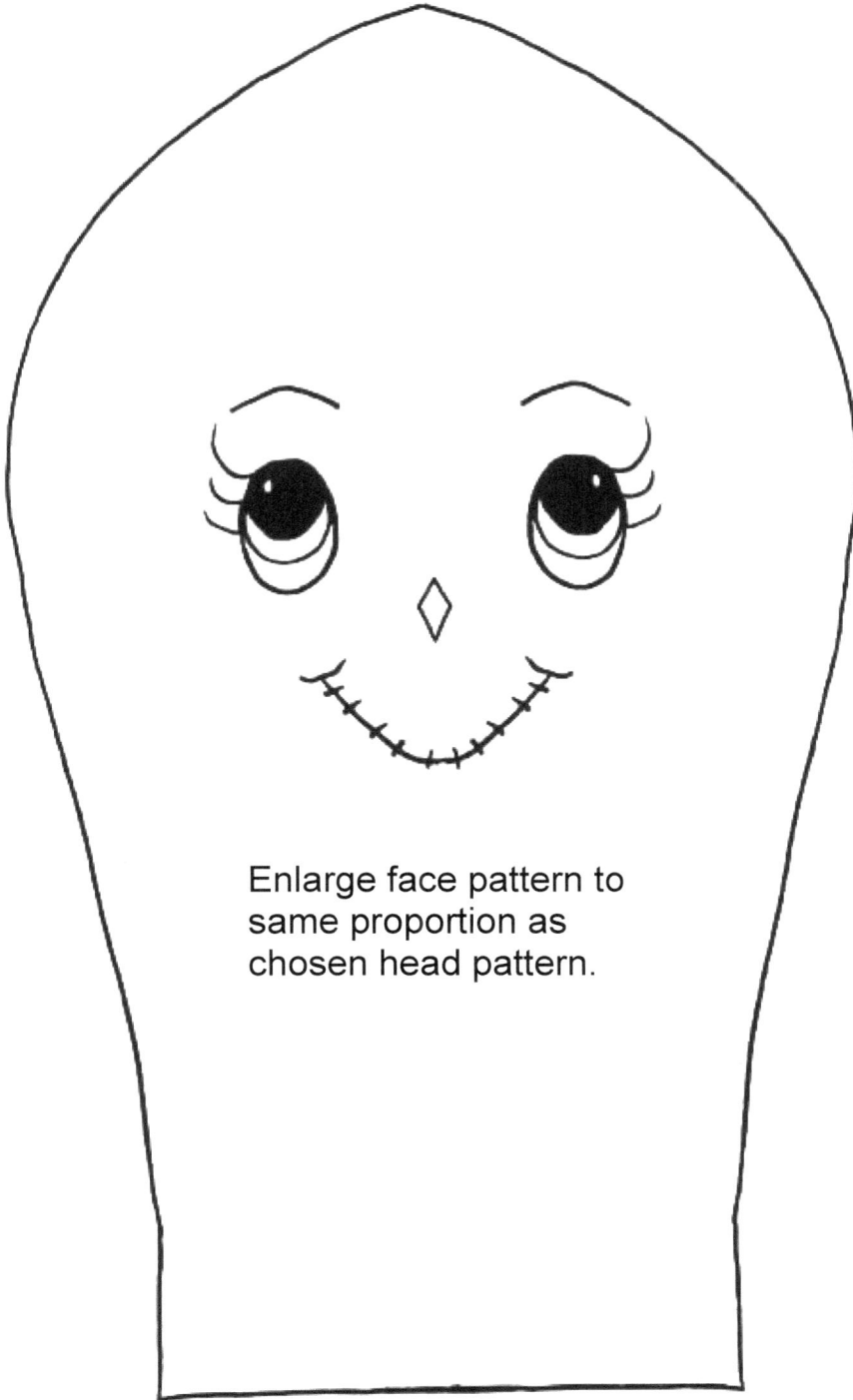

Enlarge face pattern to
same proportion as
chosen head pattern.

Patterns

Alternate faces

All of the scarecrow faces in this book are basically the same. You may want a different face. Below are a few different choices. The main thing to remember in drawing a face is to position the eyes in the **middle** of the head, **not**, toward the top.

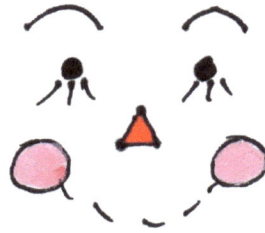

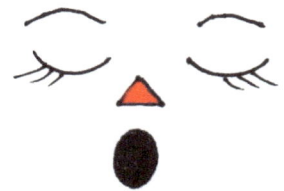

There are times when a regular scarecrow face is just not right. Below are four examples of just such a time.

A Geisha girl definitely needs Asian eyes and red lips.

Wide eyes and red ips complete the look of this sassy lady.

This farmer and his wife look good with traditional "people" faces.

This scarecrow definitely needed a cartoon face.

Buchanan Scarecrow Charities

Our History

Every fall since 2007 a group of women has decorated the downtown business area of Buchanan, Michigan with their hand-made, life-size scarecrows. The town has lovingly nicknamed these volunteers "the Scarecrow Ladies."

Initially, these lady volunteers, who were all members of the Buchanan Art Center, sold these scarecrows as a fundraiser for the Art Center. However, as the number of members grew who were not members of the Art Center, and as the group became aware of other community needs, the Scarecrow Ladies decided in late 2012 to form their own non-profit organization called Buchanan Scarecrow Charities. In this way the organization could not only provide funds for the enhancement of the Art Center and its programs but could broaden its ability to help with other charitable needs of the community.

Co-founders Carole and Mary in front of the Buchanan Art Center, 2008

Our Scarecrow Factory

A place to work and also store "scarecrow stuff" is vital to our operation. We are fortunate that Hardings Friendly Supermarket in Buchanan has allowed us to use a vacant store space in their strip mall on the outskirts of town. It is a perfect place in which to work and hold our workshops.

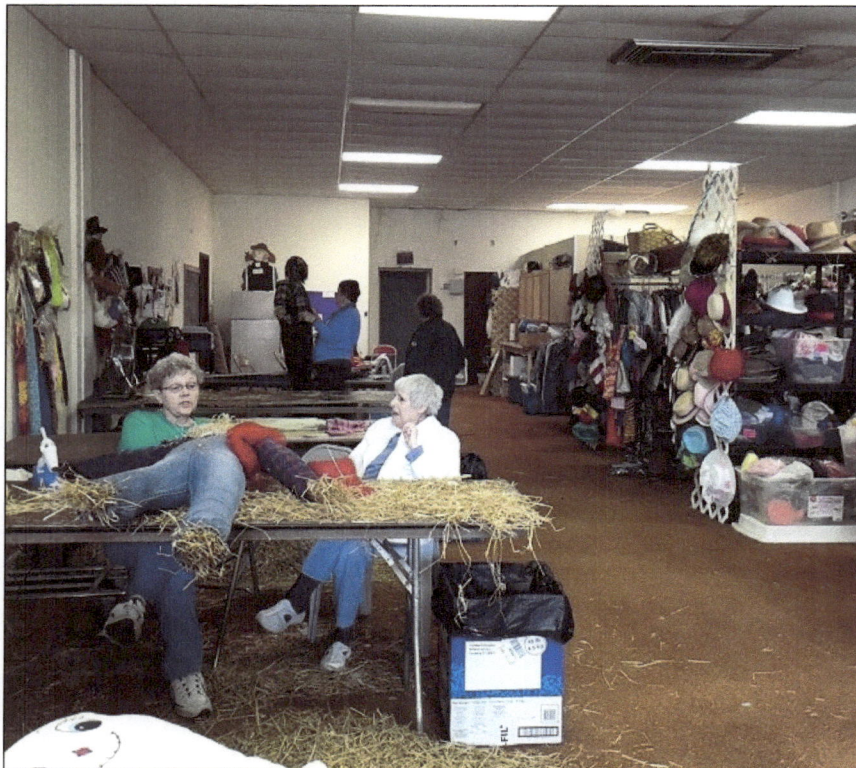

Inside, a row of long tables along one wall provides work stations for stuffing scarecrows.

In the back is a refrigerator, microwave and dining table for our lunch time needs.

Throughout the year the scarecrow ladies gather gently used clothing from garage sales, rummage sales, and second-hand clothing outlets to supply materials for making scarecrows. Also, townspeople donate items they think might be useful to us.

These clothes are then hung on clothes racks inside our scarecrow factory. These racks hold scads of bib overalls, plaid shirts, costumes, robes, and more.

Shelves hold tubs of ribbon, artificial flowers, hats, wigs, glasses, yarn hair—all the accessories needed to make our stuffed creatures. All materials are at our fingertips.

How We Work

Planning starts in late winter and by early spring construction of the scarecrows begins. Frames are made; heads are cut, sewn and painted. Then heads are stuffed, stapled and tied to wooden frames.

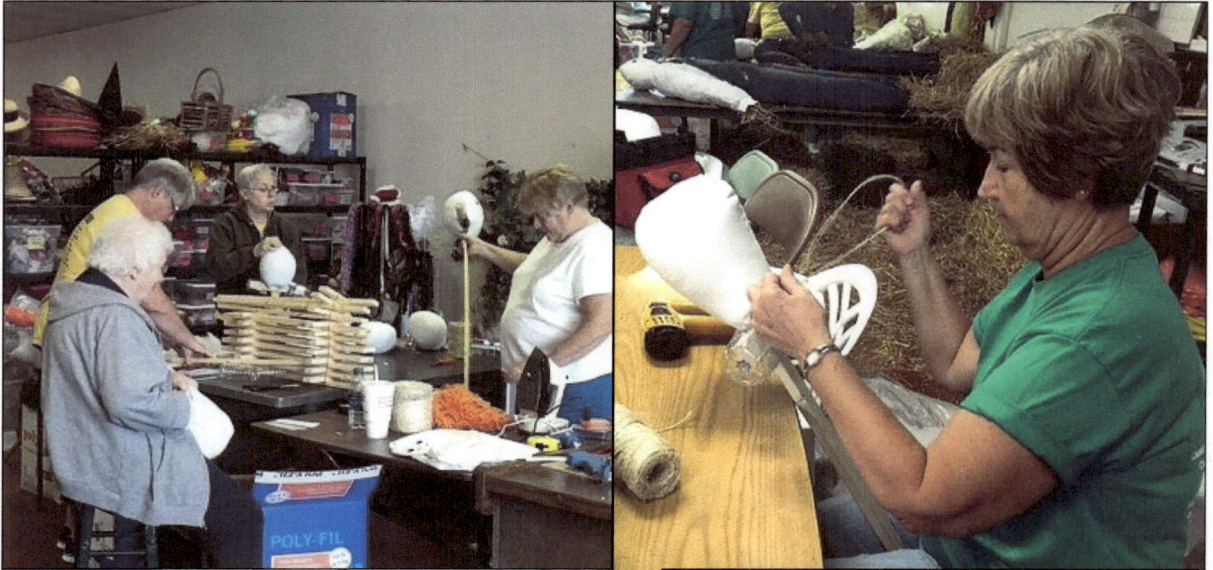

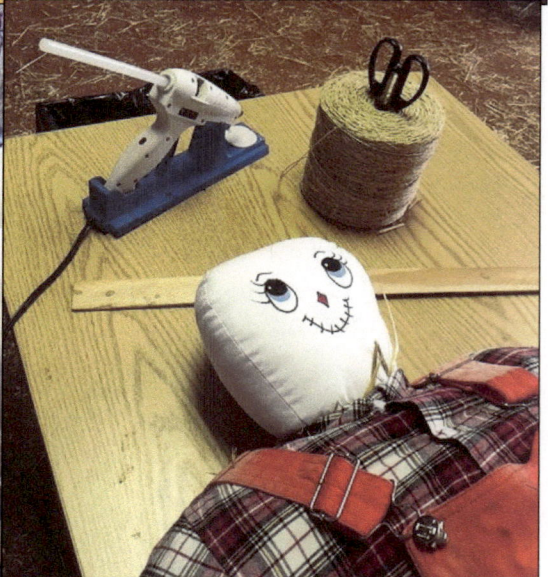

Each table work station is provided with straw, twine, a hot glue gun, scissors, wastebasket, and a stuffing stick.

Clothing is chosen, placed on wooden frames and bodies are stuffed. The creativity continues as accessories are added and the scarecrows start to "come to life" with their own personalities. The volunteers display their passion and sense of accomplishment during the making and completion of each scarecrow. It really becomes a true work of art.

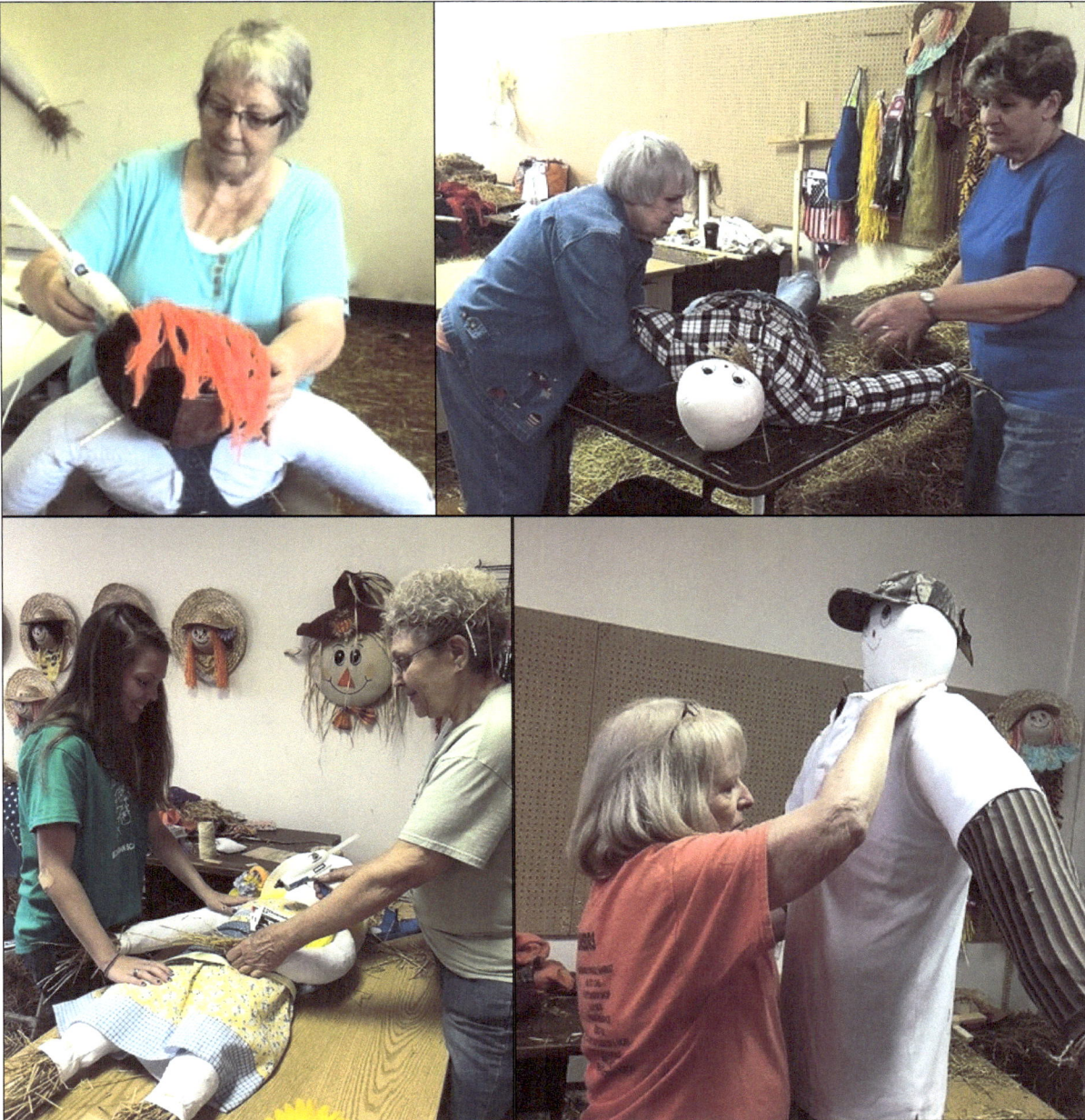

How We Work

As each scarecrow is completed, it is tagged with a number and then photographed.

The scarecrows pictured above are waiting to have their picture taken. Once photographed, each scarecrow is stored by number in a back room.

Three of our volunteers are in charge of the business signs. Pumpkin-shaped signs are cut out of wood, painted orange, and then black letters are affixed with the name of the business,

Starting the end of July, individual scarecrows are sold to area businesses. A photograph of each numbered scarecrow is placed in a photograph album which is used to sell to the local businesses.

Each business owner is able to pick the scarecrow they want to purchase from the pictures in the album. The numbering system helps keep track of each individual scarecrow.

The end of August signifies time to start setting up our scarecrow displays.

Cornstalks, which serve as backdrops for each scarecrow, are delivered by a local farmer. Several days are spent tying up cornstalks all over town; on light posts, trees, fences, railings...anywhere a scarecrow will be stationed.

Once the cornstalks are in place, completed scarecrows are taken out of the back room storage, loaded into pick-up trucks and taken to town to be put on display.

How We Work

Scarecrows are then tied to lamp posts, benches, trees, etc. along the sidewalks in town in conjunction with the orange pumpkin sign stating the business name. The sale of these scarecrows not only provides revenue for the Scarecrow Ladies charity, but also gives the business advertising for the two months the scarecrows remain in place.

The key to our success every year is the way the scarecrows are displayed. They are not simply stuffed creatures with outstretched arms. Each scarecrow is carefully posed to represent everyday people doing everyday things. One scarecrow may be perched on a bicycle as if riding down the street; another scarecrow might be hanging upside down by it's knees from a pole; another might be a mother scarecrow pushing a baby scarecrow in a stroller.

The Scarecrow Ladies expanded their unique way of posing scarecrows into creating scenes and small vignettes by using props and special clothes. Characters from history, movie stars, cartoon figures, celebrities and more are transformed into straw figures. Panoramas are made of movie scenes, popular childhood stories and even ordinary people doing ordinary things. Each year brings different characters and different scenes. People come from all over to walk the town streets, view the scarecrows, and take pictures.

Soon after Halloween the scarecrows must come down. They are untied, piled in the back of trucks and taken to a member's barn where they are stripped of their straw. Frames are recycled for another year as is clothing if still useable. All recycled materials are stored in the Scarecrow Factory to wait until spring when they again can be part of another Buchanan scarecrow display.

Our Workshops

Each year in early September the Scarecrow Ladies make additional money by conducting several "Build -A-Scarecrow" workshops for the general public. Individuals and families can attend and make their own child-size scarecrows to take home.

A scarecrow frame with stuffed head, clothes, hat, and embellishments are provided. The finished scarecrow stands a little over 4 feet tall.

Many families make this an annual affair by coming every year to make a new scarecrow to add to the collection in their yard.

Winter Carolers

The last project of the season for the Buchanan Scarecrow Ladies is to make a display of Carolers in the town Gazebo. The singing scarecrows look perfect by the lighted evergreen tree trimmed by the Buchanan Garden Club.

They look so real one can almost hear music coming from the display.

Always in Our Hearts

**Carole Hedstrom, Co-founder Buchanan Scarecrow Charities
January 18, 2016**

www.ingramcontent.com/pod-product-compliance
Lightning Source LLC
Chambersburg PA
CBHW060810090426
42737CB00002B/24